Walking Kiawah

photographs by Thalia Elizabeth Brashier
poems by Keller Cushing Freeman

To my dear Sally,
who knows how to walk the
beach and turn it into music.
With years and years of love,
Keller
October 2004

CEDAR MOUNTAIN
B O O K S

Greenville, South Carolina

Toward Kiawah

Dark old men step from shingled shacks
that straggle down Bohicket Road
toward the river.
Careful as stalking cranes,
they pick a path
along the pavement's ragged edge.

Sheltered by the shade of live oaks,
still they blink against the spatters
of September light. They carry
their heads a little forward,
their hair the gray snarled wool
of old tamed rams.

When motorists whirr past
on brief migrations to the island,
the old men raise an arm
with country courtesy,
a stiff-winged gesture
of indifferent benediction.

Autumnal Equinox

At the shore this morning
a cloud of sanderlings flew up
around me, their cries
the bitter, thin, insistent sound
of violins.

Dark-feathered bodies,
grained with white,
slit the blue September
sky into a thousand threads
of light.

Walking Kiawah

We walked the narrow spit of land,
a track of sand and oyster shells
thrown out like a line
between the river and a marsh
where chalk-white egrets stood
proud as popes under a Sistine sky.

It was October. You touched my arm,
then pointed toward the riverbank.
I looked, thinking to see
a great blue heron or wood ibis,
solitary, motionless,
inaccessible as saints.

Instead I saw a burning bush
shimmering with tongues of fire:
burnt sienna, umber, terracotta.
The flames took flight,
became a tapestry of butterflies,
undulant against the arching air.

Winter Solstice

Always returning to this ocean,
always coming home
to the vast indifference of the sea.
The distant cry of cormorants
echoes my cry for healing.

But there is no comfort here.
Instead, a scouring of wind, salt, sand,
until there's nothing left
but white bones bleached of memory.

New Year's Day

The river marsh in winter
mirrors back a low, bruised sky.
Snowy egrets haunt the shallows
where snow so seldom falls.

A January wind
winds severe through limbs
of live oaks, catches
in a net of long-leaf pine.

As if seeking shelter
from the certain storm,
palm fronds stutter, scratch
against a shutter.

On the bare shore
of this new year I hesitate,
wait for some sense of what will be
required, then turn to face the sea.

By Owl Light

White-tailed deer anticipate the dawn.
A pair of fawns, having lost the russet coats
of summer, move like gray shadows
against a marsh grass monotone.

Almost invisible, their mother waits
at the base of a barren cedar.
The tree, no longer evergreen,
still provides a meager shelter
from the morning winds.

Low tide an hour past,
the misted river rises to erase
narrow island mounds of oyster beds.
At the first hint of light
a great horned owl descends
to command the cedar's highest limb.

Large as any hawk, this raptor
has few enemies to fear.
Deliberately it scans the margin
of the marsh for prey, then turns
its fierce face toward the winter window
where I watch. Confronted,
I am first to look away.

Vernal Equinox

Black patent leather grackles
glint and crackle in a citrus sun's
electric dazzle.

At last it's over,
the senseless sentence of gray days,
the rain cage of a Southern winter.

A ripple of feathers signals
the time for flight. Sharp wings
scissor the sky, releasing light.

The T'ai Chi Master

The slate-blue striated sky of April
echoes off the river surface.
At first I fail to see him, so perfectly attuned
are his feathers to all the morning colors.

Then he turns his head toward shore,
presenting an exotic mask of black and white,
the elaborated eyes of an actor
in some archaic Chinese play.

Incoming tides, rich with flurries
of metallic fish, wash through his legs,
sway new-green reeds that etch
their hatchmarks on the marsh.

The great blue heron, with a thrust
certain as a dancer's arm, executes the placement
of his head in profile. His sinuous neck undulates
to undergird his head. He advances one careful length

of leg. Then strikes. I am reminded his black beak
is not a simple brush stroke, but a blade.
T'ai Chi, no discipline for dance,
prepares its adepts for the art of war.

Summer Solstice

The shorebirds lose no time.
They know the tide reclaims what it has given.
They pick out a persistent present tense,
since nothing can hold fast against tomorrow.

I know the tide reclaims what it has given,
for I, too, live on sufferance like the shorebirds,
since nothing can hold fast against tomorrow
and every love conceals the seeds of loss.

I have no choice. I live on sufferance,
forage every tide-mark like the shorebirds.
Since every love conceals the seeds of loss,
my days are driven by persistent hunger.

I forage every tide-mark like the shorebirds,
in search of love beyond the reach of water,
driven by this old persistent hunger,
observing that the shorebirds lose no time.

Island Native

Emerging from the summer marsh
a terrapin, squat legs bowed
into parentheses, shuffles
like a tired old man in bedroom shoes
onto the oozing asphalt road.

The creature's head, barely extended
from the awning shade of its mottled shell,
turns slowly left, then right,
then left again.

Crossing a road holds dangers
unpremeditated when the Mesozoic brain
took shape a hundred million years ago.
Is it some premonition of the Automotive Age?

Or the treachery of tar pits
at La Brea that makes the terrapin
pause, take stock, execute
a cumbersome half turn, and then retreat
to the primal sanctuary of pluff mud?

Leaving Kiawah

Take Kiawah away with you.
Breathe its stringent air into every cell.
Remember that its sea taste
salts our blood, our tears.

Sense the certain rhythm of its tides
repeating in your pulse.
Leave this island
radiant with light.

Although sometimes in different versions, these poems originally appeared in the following publications:

45/96: The Ninety-Six Sampler of South Carolina Poetry (Ninety-Six Press, 1994): "Toward Kiawah" (as "Johns Island").

Walking Like a Waterspider (Ninety-Six Press, 1996): "The T'ai Chi Master."

Trespass of Venus (Emrys Press, 2000): "Autumnal Equinox," "Winter Solstice," "Summer Solstice."

Book design by David M. Starzec

Library of Congress Catalog Card Number: 2004111511
ISBN 0-9760217-0-6